W9-BAF-376

CHILDREN 523.8 MILLER 2011
Miller, Ron
Seven wonders beyond the
    solar system

Central   07/27/2011

CENTRAL LIBRARY

7

Seven Wonders

Seven Wonders beyond the
SOLAR SYSTEM

Ron Miller

TWENTY-FIRST CENTURY BOOKS

Minneapolis

To Zara Hickman

Copyright © 2011 by Ron Miller

All rights reserved. International copyright secured. No part of this book may be reproduced, stored in a retrieval system, or transmitted in any form or by any means—electronic, mechanical, photocopying, recording, or otherwise—without the prior written permission of Lerner Publishing Group, Inc., except for the inclusion of brief quotations in an acknowledged review.

Twenty-First Century Books
A division of Lerner Publishing Group, Inc.
241 First Avenue North
Minneapolis, MN 55401 U.S.A.

Website address: www.lernerbooks.com

Library of Congress Cataloging-in-Publication Data

Miller, Ron, 1947-
    Seven wonders beyond the solar system / by Ron Miller.
        p.   cm. — (Seven wonders)
    Includes bibliographical references and index.
    ISBN 978–0–7613–5454–3 (lib. bdg. : alk. paper)
    1. Nebulae—Juvenile literature. 2. Extrasolar planets—Juvenile literature. 3. Solar system—Miscellanea—Juvenile literature. I. Title.
    QB855.2.M55 2011
    523.8—dc22   2010028446

Manufactured in the United States of America
1 – DP – 12/31/10

Contents

1
2
3
4
5
6
7

*P*EOPLE LOVE TO MAKE LISTS OF THE BIGGEST AND THE BEST. ALMOST TWENTY-FIVE HUNDRED YEARS AGO, A GREEK WRITER NAMED HERODOTUS MADE A LIST OF THE MOST AWESOME THINGS EVER BUILT BY PEOPLE. THE LIST INCLUDED BUILDINGS, STATUES, AND OTHER OBJECTS THAT WERE LARGE, WONDROUS, AND IMPRESSIVE. LATER, OTHER WRITERS ADDED NEW ITEMS TO THE LIST. WRITERS EVENTUALLY AGREED ON A FINAL LIST. IT WAS CALLED THE SEVEN WONDERS OF THE ANCIENT WORLD.

The list became so famous that people began imitating it. They made other lists of wonders. They listed the Seven Wonders of the Modern World and the Seven Wonders of the Middle Ages. People also made lists of wonders of science and technology.

OUT OF THIS WORLD

But Earth isn't the only place with wonders. Our planet shares the universe with many other wondrous places. Earth is one of eight planets that orbit, or circle, the Sun. The Sun and everything that circles it, including the planets and their moons, make up a place called the solar system. Beyond the solar system, the universe holds billions and billions of stars. These stars are all suns, similar to the Sun. What worlds might circle them? What wonders might they contain?

On a cloudless night, far from city lights, you can see countless stars in the sky. Each of these stars is a sun, similar to our Sun.

BEYOND THE SOLAR SYSTEM

Seven Wonders beyond the Solar System will take you on an amazing journey to faraway places. On this journey, we'll learn about stars that are being born and stars that have already died. We'll explore very tiny stars, as well as stars as big as our whole solar system. We'll learn how astronomers, or space scientists, look for new stars and planets. We'll even join astronomers as they search for life on other planets. We'll also examine giant clusters of stars called galaxies. We'll learn how galaxies cluster together to create the biggest thing there is—the universe itself. Read on to visit this fascinating world billions of miles away in space.

1 THE *Tarantula* NEBULA

The Tarantula Nebula is a birthplace for new stars.

$\mathcal{S}$TARS ARE HUGE BALLS OF GAS IN SPACE THAT

GIVE OFF LIGHT, HEAT, AND OTHER KINDS OF ENERGY. THE SUN (*BELOW*)

IS A STAR. THE UNIVERSE CONTAINS BILLIONS AND BILLIONS OF STARS.

Like people, stars are born. Unlike people, stars are born inside clouds. The clouds that give birth to stars are vast areas of dust, gas, and ice in space. Most of the gas is hydrogen.

The universe is filled with millions of such clouds. Some are small, and some are enormous. These clouds are called nebulae. *Nebula* (referring to only one cloud) means "cloud" in Latin. The Tarantula Nebula is the biggest nebula anyone knows about. It is trillions of miles wide.

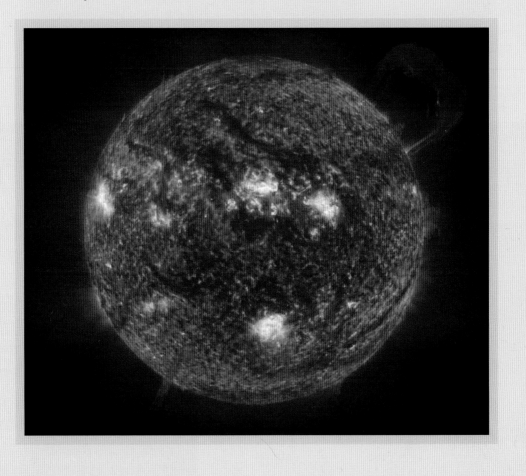

THE SEEDS OF A STAR

All substances, including the gases inside nebulae, are made of tiny particles. Some of the smallest particles are called atoms. Groups of atoms are called molecules. Inside a nebula, molecules are spread very far apart. But the molecules have gravity, the force by which one substance attracts another. So the molecules inside a nebula attract one another. They start to drift together. The nebula begins to contract, or shrink. The contraction begins where the gas and the dust are a bit denser than elsewhere in the nebula.

Once the contraction starts, it cannot stop. Molecules of dust and gas start drifting toward the center of the nebula, which has more material and therefore more gravity. As the gravity increases, more particles come together. The molecules bump against one another. Every time this happens, a little heat is created.

As the nebula continues to contract, its molecules continue to move closer together. More and more molecules bump against one another. The nebula grows even warmer. Eventually the dust and the gas start sticking together in a lump. The lump grows larger and larger.

This lump of contracting gas and dust is just a very small part of a much larger nebula. Other small knots of contracting gas and dust might also be

Nebulae glow with light from new young stars.

SEE FOR *Yourself*

Gases grow hotter when they are compressed, or squeezed together. You can see this process for yourself by inflating a bicycle tire. As you press more air (a gas) into the small space of the tire, you'll feel the tire get hotter. The same heating occurs when gases squeeze together inside a nebula.

"Nothing else can be so pretty! A cluster of vapor, the cream of the milky way, a sort of celestial cheese, churned into light."

—*Benjamin Disraeli, British political leader, remarking on the creation of a star, 1847*

forming at other places in the nebula. The small knots might eventually become stars.

A Star Is Born

At the center of the nebula, the gas and the dust become very dense, or tightly packed together. The center grows hotter as more and more gas and dust fall into it. As more material falls in, the gravity at the center of the nebula grows greater. The more gravity the nebula has, the more tightly packed the material becomes. In just one year, a nebula can shrink to one ten-thousandth of its original size.

Soon the nebula reaches 3,000°F (1,650°C). This is hot enough to vaporize, or turn into gas, any grains of ice or dust the nebula contains. The densely packed nebula begins to glow dim red, like a hot coal.

As the core of the nebula continues to heat up, the nucleus (center) of each hydrogen atom presses against the one next to it. The atoms fuse, or stick together, like two balls of clay being squished together. When hydrogen atoms fuse, the hydrogen turns into a different kind of gas, helium. The process of hydrogen becoming helium is called nuclear fusion. This process creates vast amounts of energy.

Fusion is not easy to achieve. It requires tremendous pressure and a very high

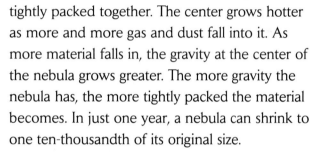

High *Power*

Fusion creates huge amounts of energy. Every 2.2 pounds (1 kilogram) of hydrogen that turns into helium inside a star creates about 400 trillion trillion watts of energy. That's enough energy to light 10 trillion trillion 40-watt lightbulbs.

temperature. It takes 10 million years of contraction for a nebula to reach the temperature needed for fusion to begin. As soon as the spark of fusion is lit, the nebula stops contracting. It becomes a full-fledged sun. It begins running on the energy produced by fusion. A star has been born.

THE BIGGEST STAR FACTORY

If you live in the Southern Hemisphere (southern half of Earth), you can look into the sky at night and see the Tarantula Nebula. It is the largest "star nursery" anyone knows about. Hundreds and perhaps even thousands of new stars are being born within it.

Powerful telescopes in the Southern Hemisphere allow us to see the young stars inside the Tarantula Nebula.

The nebula looks a little like a tarantula, a big hairy spider.

To the naked eye, the Tarantula Nebula doesn't look like much. It looks like a faint, fuzzy blob of light in the constellation (star group) Dorado. When seen through a telescope, however, the Tarantula Nebula looks like a swirling mass of red and green gases. Its shape resembles a tarantula, a large hairy spider.

A light-year is the distance light travels in one year. Light travels 186,000 miles (300,000 kilometers) per second. So 1 light-year equals about 5.88 trillion miles (9.46 trillion km). The Tarantula Nebula is 170,000 light-years away from Earth. So light from the Tarantula Nebula takes 170,000 years to reach Earth.

At the center of the Tarantula Nebula is a small cluster of young stars. Energy from these stars makes the nebula glow brightly, much like electricity passing through the tube of a neon sign makes the gas inside it glow.

The Hubble Space Telescope, which orbits Earth, took this picture of the Orion Nebula in Orion's sword (see illustration on page 27). The nebula contains more than three thousand stars.

"[The Tarantula Nebula] has a sparkling stellar centerpiece: the most spectacular cluster of massive stars in our cosmic neighborhood of about 25 galaxies."

—*HubbleSite, Space Telescope Science Institute, 2001*

THE ORION
Nebula

One of the nearest nebulae to Earth is the Orion Nebula. It is in the constellation Orion (see page 27). The nebula is visible to the naked eye as a faint patch of light. It looks smaller than your little fingernail. When seen through a small telescope, it looks like a glowing pink cloud. The Orion Nebula is just 1,500 to 1,600 light-years away from Earth. This is one hundred times closer to Earth than the Tarantula Nebula.

The Orion Nebula is also much smaller than the Tarantula Nebula. It is about 30 light-years wide. The Tarantula Nebula is 1,000 light-years wide. If the Tarantula Nebula were as close to Earth as the Orion Nebula is, the Tarantula Nebula would appear to fill almost one-quarter of the sky. It would even be visible in daylight.

Throughout the rest of the nebula are dark knots of contracting dust and gas. These are places where new stars are being created. Eventually the knots will become dense and hot enough to trigger a fusion reaction. When this happens, each one will become a new star.

Of all the wonders of the universe, places like the Tarantula Nebula are among the most exciting. It is there that astronomers can witness the birth of new stars. Understanding this process helps us understand the birth of our own star, the Sun.

2 THE *Crab* NEBULA

Astronomers combined different kinds of images to create this image of the Crab Nebula.

SCATTERED THROUGHOUT SPACE ARE HUNDREDS OF BEAUTIFUL NEBULAE. THEY COME IN EVERY IMAGINABLE SHAPE AND COLOR. THE COLORS COME FROM GLOWING GASES WITHIN THE NEBULAE. ONE OF THE MOST BEAUTIFUL AND MOST FAMOUS NEBULAE IS THE CRAB NEBULA. UNLIKE THE TARANTULA NEBULA, WHICH IS A PLACE WHERE STARS ARE BORN, THE CRAB NEBULA IS THE RESULT OF A STAR THAT DIED.

The Crab Nebula is all that remains of an exploded star.

Sometimes a very large star explodes. When it does, it bursts into a supernova. In this titanic explosion, the star suddenly flares with a billion times the brightness of the Sun. At the same time, the star's atmosphere, or surrounding layer of gases, blasts out into space. The explosion looks like a beautiful shell of glowing gas. For a few days, the supernova outshines the combined stars of its entire galaxy.

BANG!

Scientists aren't entirely sure what causes a star to explode. But they do know about two types of supernovas. One type of supernova requires two stars that

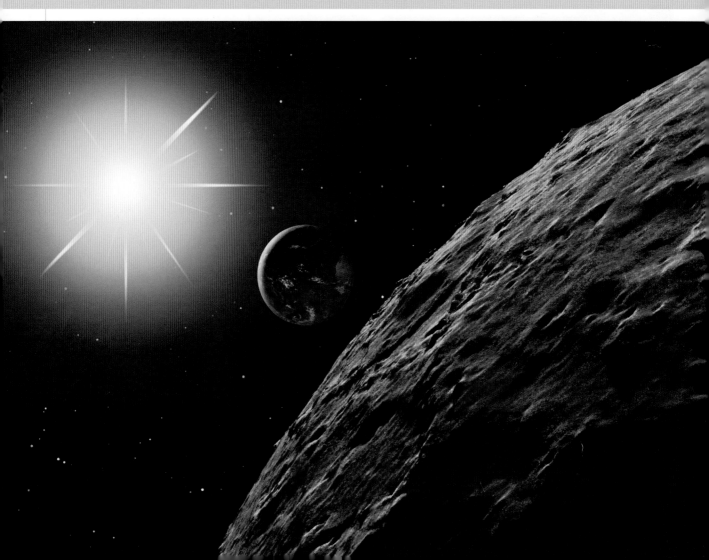

This painting shows what a supernova would look like if viewed from Earth's Moon.

TELESCOPE *Time Machines*

Telescopes are time machines. They allow us to look into the past. Why and how? Because of the speed of light. When you see an object in the sky, you do not see it as it looks in the twenty-first century. You see it as it looked when the light reaching your eyes left the object. The Sun is 93 million miles (150 million km) from Earth. Light takes about seven minutes to travel this distance. So when you look at the Sun, you are seeing it as it was seven minutes ago. If the Sun were to suddenly go out, you would not know it until seven minutes later. The nearest star to our solar system is Alpha Centauri. It is 4.3 light-years away. We see that star not as it looks today but as it looked 4.3 years ago. The farther objects are from Earth, the farther we are looking into their past. The galaxies we see that are billions of light-years away appear as they looked billions of years in the past. We will never know what they look like in our time.

orbit one another. One has to be a very large star, much bigger than the Sun. The other needs to be a white dwarf. A white dwarf is a remnant of a burned-out star.

White dwarfs are tiny stars, not much larger than Earth. But they contain a great amount of mass. *Mass* is another word for the amount of stuff something is made of. A feather pillow weighing 1 pound (0.5 kilograms) has as much mass as a brick weighing 1 pound. But the brick is denser than the pillow because its mass is tightly packed into a smaller space.

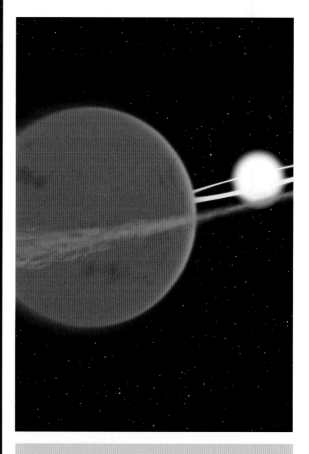

With its great mass, a white dwarf might pull gases from a nearby larger star.

A white dwarf can be as massive (have as much mass) as the Sun. With so much mass crammed into such a small space, white dwarfs are very dense. Denser objects have more gravity than objects with less density.

When a white dwarf and a larger star orbit each other, the white dwarf's powerful gravity pulls on the larger star. Gases from the big star flow to the white dwarf. Eventually, too much mass builds up on the white dwarf. The excess mass causes the white dwarf to blow up. The entire star suddenly disappears in a single, incredible explosion.

A star that has too much mass to remain stable, or unchanging, can lead to the second type of supernova. Such a star is typically more than six times as massive as the Sun. When the massive star gets old and runs out of gaseous fuel to burn, it collapses. This collapse creates tremendous pressure in the core of the star. This pressure can trigger violent fusion reactions. They can cause the star to explode into a supernova. After a supernova, only the tiny core of the star remains.

THE GHOSTS OF STARS

The night sky is filled with the remains of supernovas. They are colorful clouds of dust and gas left over from the explosions. No two are exactly alike. One of the most beautiful such clouds is the Crab Nebula. Through a telescope, it looks like a lacy burst of multicolored strands.

The Crab Nebula is the result of a star that was seen to explode in the year 1054. It actually exploded sixty-five hundred years earlier. But the Crab Nebula is 6,500 light-years from Earth. So it took light from the explosion sixty-five hundred years to reach Earth.

In July of 1054, Chinese astronomers noted the appearance of a "guest star" (a temporary star) in the constellation Taurus. People could see the guest star in broad daylight for three weeks. They saw it at night for two years before it finally faded away. The Chinese astronomers didn't know it, but they had witnessed the supernova that created the Crab Nebula.

Native Americans in Chaco Canyon in New Mexico may also have witnessed this impressive sight. A pictograph (rock painting) there appears to show a new star. It is shown near a crescent moon. The crescent moon would have appeared in the sky very close to the supernova in July 1054.

Guest Stars

In addition to the Crab Nebula, people have seen other "guest stars" over the centuries. In November 1572, Danish astronomer Tycho Brahe *(below)* noticed a new star in the constellation Cassiopeia. He didn't know it, but his "new star" was really an exploding star. He wrote a book about what he saw. The book's title was *De nova stella* (about the new star). After that, astronomers called any exploding star a nova.

In the 1930s, astronomers discovered stars that exploded with special violence. They called these explosions supernovas. In 1987 astronomers saw a supernova in the Large Magellanic Cloud. This small galaxy orbits our own galaxy, the Milky Way. The explosion was the first one in almost four hundred years that could be seen without a telescope.

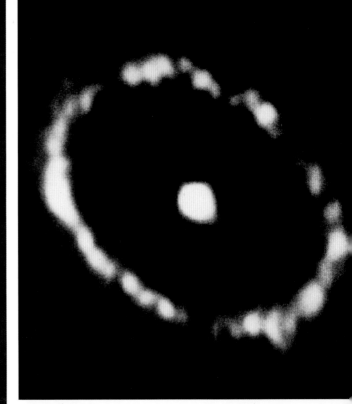

Top: *This supernova appeared in the skies in 1987. The ring surrounding it is gas being expelled by the explosion.*

Bottom: *Astronomers think that the star in the lower left of this pictograph from Chaco Canyon in New Mexico is a supernova that appeared in 1054.*

In modern times, almost one thousand years later, the Crab Nebula is one of the most beautiful objects in the night sky. You can easily see it with even a small telescope. It is a glowing cloud of dust and gas. It looks like a puff of smoke left behind after a firecracker explodes. Astronomers in the nineteenth century gave the nebula its name. They thought it resembled the claw of a crab.

The Crab Nebula is huge. It spans almost 10 light-years, or 60 trillion miles (97 trillion km). And it's growing bigger, much like a cloud of smoke that billows out after an explosion. In fact, astronomers can see changes in the nebula as it grows larger from year to year.

THE END
of a Star

In a typical galaxy, such as our own, only about one star per century ends its life as a supernova. Some stars end their lives as novas. Novas are much less powerful explosions than supernovas. But even these explosions are rare. The Sun, a fairly typical star, is the kind of star that will never explode. Instead, the Sun will eventually swell to many times its present size. Eventually, as its gaseous fuel runs out, it will begin to shrink. At the end of its life, it may become a tiny white dwarf.

A supernova created the Crab Nebula. The supernova occurred about seventy-five hundred years ago. Its light reached Earth in 1054.

"[Novas] offer to the mind a phenomenon more surprising, and less explicable, than almost any other in the science of astronomy."

—*George Adams, British scientist, 1794*

MORE NEBULAE

Nebulae take many different shapes and forms. For instance, the Helix Nebula looks like a giant eyeball. It has a colored center, like the iris of a human eye, with a bright round area surrounding it. It is really a round shell of glowing gas.

Unlike the Crab Nebula, the Helix Nebula did not come from a supernova explosion. Instead, the Helix was created by the gas of a dying star. When a star gets old, it might swell up like a gigantic balloon and then suddenly shrink to a very tiny size. When this happens, the star throws off a shell of gas. The hollow shell expands like a soap bubble. The tiny remnant of the original star lights up the bubble, causing it to glow.

The Helix Nebula is much smaller than the Crab Nebula. The Crab is more than 10 light-years wide. The Helix spans only 2.5 light-years. Nebulae such as the Helix are called planetary nebulae because they are round like planets. Most planetary nebulae look like bright rings.

The Veil Nebula is one of the most beautiful nebulae of all. It is a collection of graceful arcs of gas. They glow pink, green, and blue. The nebula looks like the faint wisps of smoke after a candle has been blown out. It is all that remains of a supernova that exploded thousands of years ago. After many more thousands of years, the Veil Nebula will spread out so far and become so thin that it will all but disappear.

Some nebulae do not shine at all. They are made of dark dust and gas. They have no inner or nearby star to make them glow. These are called dark nebulae. You can see them only against a background of stars or bright nebulae. A famous one is called the Coal Sack. It sits right in front of a bright region of the Milky Way. It looks like a big dark patch with no stars. Another dark nebula is the Horsehead Nebula. It is easy to see how it got its name. It looks a lot like a horse's head.

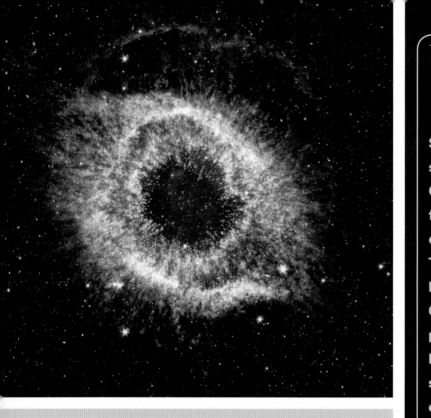

Above: *The Helix Nebula looks a lot like a human eye.*
Below: *The Veil Nebula looks like a lacy veil.*

FAR TOO *Small*

Some very large nebulae, such as the Tarantula and Orion nebulae, are star factories. They are gigantic clouds of dust and gas. They are big enough to hold hundreds of new stars. The Crab Nebula is just a little puff of smoke by comparison. It is all that's left of a single star. It is much too small to create new stars.

The dark Horsehead Nebula does not give off its own light.

THREE CATEGORIES

Astronomers label nebulae according to how or whether they glow. A reflection nebula reflects light from a nearby star. It gives off no light of its own. An emission nebula shines because energy from a nearby star or a star inside the nebula causes gases in the nebula to glow. An emission nebula gives off its own light. The Orion Nebula and the Crab Nebula are examples of emission nebulae. The third type of nebula is a dark nebula. It gives off no light. A good example is the Coal Sack Nebula.

"Some of the most interesting clouds [nebulae] are the densest—huge black monsters that lurk in space, almost invisible except for the fact that they block the light of stars behind them."

—William K. Hartmann, American astronomer, 1987

3 THE MYSTERIOUS *Pulsing Star*

This illustration of a pulsar shows the different types of invisible particles that pulsars emit. The purple lines are magnetic field lines. The red and white beams are pulses of radiation from the magnetic poles.

*P*ULSARS ARE AMONG THE MOST FASCINATING OBJECTS IN THE UNIVERSE. THEY ARE TINY, FAST-SPINNING STARS THAT EMIT POWERFUL BEAMS OF RADIO ENERGY. RADIO ENERGY IS THE SAME KIND OF ENERGY BROADCAST BY RADIO AND TV STATIONS.

Pulsars were originally ordinary stars. But they were very big ordinary stars. The typical pulsar probably started out as a star at least eight times more massive than the Sun. Then the star exploded in a supernova. During the explosion, most of the star was blown away. Nothing was left but a tiny core. The core was a neutron star.

The pulsar PSR B1257+12 has several planets. This illustration shows the pulsar (center) *and two planets as seen from a third planet.*

> *"Most supernova explosions leave a stellar cinder, the exhausted inner core, which promptly collapses to form a neutron star."*
>
> —William K. Hartmann, American astronomer, 1987

NEUTRON STARS

Neutron stars are the smallest and densest stars known to astronomers. The typical neutron star is only 6 to 12 miles (10 to 20 km) across. But it is still very massive. A neutron star may have as much mass as the Sun. So much mass crammed into such a small space makes neutron stars very heavy. A teaspoon of material from a neutron star would weigh 2 billion tons (1.8 billion metric tons) on Earth.

This illustration shows asteroids and meteoroids surrounding a tiny neutron star. One of them has crashed into the star's solid surface.

Constellations

People sometimes look at the stars and see patterns. In earlier centuries, people thought that some groups of stars looked like the outlines of human figures, animals, and other objects. People named the groups after the objects or figures they envisioned. For instance, people thought that one group of stars looked like a big drinking cup. They named that group the Big Dipper. They thought another group looked like a hunter. They named the group Orion *(below)*, after a hunter in Greek mythology. Groups of stars named by people in earlier times are called constellations.

CONSTELLATION ORION

Betelgeuse

Orion Nebula

Rigel

Because of the great mass, the gravity on the surface of a neutron star is extremely powerful. It is millions of times stronger than Earth's gravity. If you could land on a neutron star, the star's gravity would pull you to the surface with great force. You would be flattened thinner than a sheet of paper. Any mountains on the neutron star would be flattened to only a fraction of an inch high.

Unlike ordinary stars, neutron stars have a solid crust, or outer covering. This crust is made of iron and electrons. Electrons are atomic particles, or particles found inside atoms. Scientists think that neutron stars might have a liquid interior, also made of atomic particles, under their crust.

The temperature at the very center of a neutron star can be 180 million°F (100 million°C). By comparison, the surface of the Sun is only about 10,000°F (5,500°C). The crust of a neutron star is also extremely hot. It might be 90,000°F (50,000°C). But a neutron star's tiny size means that it shines a million times fainter than the Sun.

All stars rotate, or spin. The smaller a star is, the faster it rotates. You can see this process yourself by watching figure skaters. When their arms are extended, figure skaters spin slowly. But as skaters draw their arms in toward their bodies, they spin faster and faster. Because neutron stars are so small, they rotate very rapidly.

PULSARS

Some neutron stars give off pulses of radio energy as they spin. Scientists call these pulsing stars, or pulsars for short. Pulsars rotate incredibly rapidly. They spin hundreds of times per second. Some pulsars rotate *thousands* of times per second. When seen through a telescope, the surface of a pulsar is usually nothing but a blur.

In addition to radio energy, pulsars give off much more powerful kinds of energy. One type is radiation. Radiation is the kind of energy used in X-rays. A pulsar's radiation and radio energy are invisible. But beams of visible light shine from a pulsar's north and south poles.

Every once in a while, the outer crust of a pulsar cracks. Scientists call this event a starquake. During a

LITTLE GREEN *Men*

British astronomers Jocelyn Bell and Anthony Hewish *(below)* discovered pulsars in 1967. At first the perfect, regular pulses puzzled the astronomers. The pulses were like nothing else found in nature. Were they signals from an alien civilization? Bell and Hewish half-jokingly referred to the source of the pulses as LGM. That's short for "little green men."

"Were these pulsations man-made, but by man from another civilization?"

—*Jocelyn Bell, a British astronomer who discovered pulsars, 1977*

starquake, the pulsar's rotation speeds up slightly. The pulsar also gives off an intense burst of radiation.

A Pulsar and Its Planets

The beam of radio energy from a pulsar sweeps the sky like a beam of light from a lighthouse. Just as light from a lighthouse seems to flash or blink every time it swings toward us, the pulsar's beam of radio energy seems to pulse every time.

Most pulsars have a steady pulse. But in 1992, scientists noticed that a pulsar named PSR B1257+12 had an uneven pulse. Sometimes the pulse came a fraction of a second late. Other times it came a fraction of a second early. Scientists knew that only one thing could be causing this irregular pulse. The pulsar must have planets orbiting it. Gravity from the planets pulls the pulsar first one way and then the other. This pull affects the timing of the pulses.

This illustration shows Pulsar PSR 1257+12 flashing through the atmosphere of a planet orbiting it.

Above: *Galileo Galilei was the the first person to use a telescope to study the sky.* Below: *The Hubble Space Telescope is one of several telescopes orbiting Earth.*

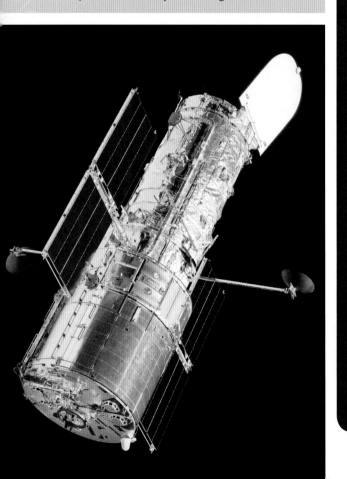

ASTRONOMERS and *Their Tools*

Astronomers study the stars and the planets. The word *astronomer* comes from *astron*, the Greek word for "star."

The first astronomers studied the stars using only their eyes. In 1608 a Dutch lens maker named Johannes Lipperhey made the first telescope. Two years later, an Italian scientist named Galileo Galilei built a telescope. He used it to study the sky. People soon built larger and more powerful telescopes. They used them to see objects in space that are invisible to the human eye alone.

In modern times, astronomers use extremely powerful telescopes to study space. Some telescopes have built-in cameras. Some telescopes are attached to satellites, or spacecraft that orbit Earth. One of the most powerful orbiting telescopes is the Hubble Space Telescope. The United States launched the Hubble into space in 1990. Far above the clouds and pollution of Earth's atmosphere, the Hubble and other orbiting telescopes capture extremely clear images from space.

Some special telescopes can "see" light and energy that are invisible to the human eye. With these telescopes, astronomers can study objects they would not be able to see otherwise.

This illustration shows PSR B1257+12 and the planets and their moons that surround it.

Astronomers think that at least four planets orbit PSR B1257+12. One planet, about three times the mass of Earth, takes about ninety-eight days to circle the pulsar. Another planet, about three and one-half times the size of Earth, orbits in just over sixty-six days. Both planets are about the same distance from the pulsar that Mercury is from the Sun. That's about 36 million miles (58 million km). A third planet orbits less than 18 million miles (29 million km) from the pulsar. It is a very small planet. It is about one-fifth the size of Pluto, a dwarf planet in our own solar system. Scientists think that at least one other planet orbits the pulsar.

PSR B12157+12's planets are probably very rugged places. They are most likely balls of rock and metal. They are cold, frozen worlds. Their only light comes from the dim glow of the pulsar.

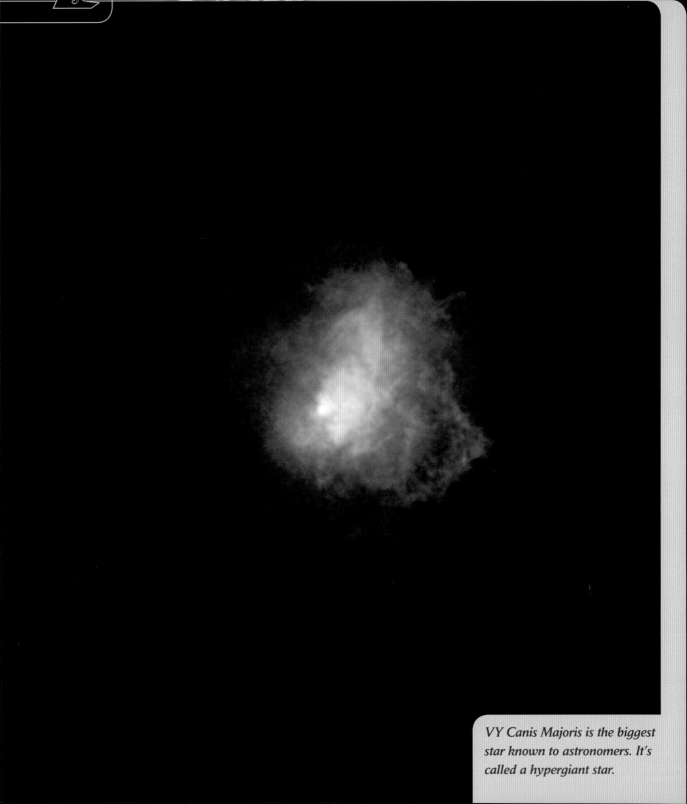

VY Canis Majoris is the biggest star known to astronomers. It's called a hypergiant star.

$\mathcal{S}$TARS COME IN ALL SIZES. MANY ARE MUCH SMALLER THAN THE SUN. FOR INSTANCE, WHITE DWARFS MIGHT BE NOT MUCH LARGER THAN EARTH, OR ONE HUNDRED TIMES SMALLER THAN THE SUN. ON THE OTHER END OF THE SCALE ARE THE GIANT STARS. THE SUPERGIANT RIGEL IS A BRIGHT STAR IN THE CONSTELLATION ORION. IT IS TWENTY-FIVE TIMES LARGER THAN THE SUN. BETELGEUSE, ANOTHER STAR IN ORION, IS NEARLY ONE THOUSAND TIMES LARGER THAN THE SUN.

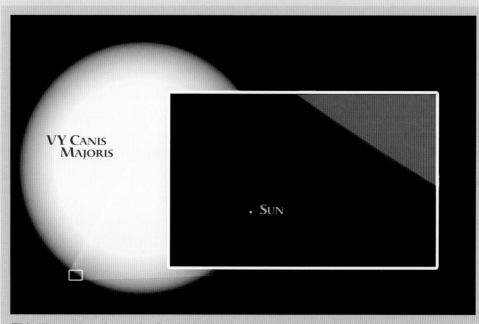

VY CANIS
MAJORIS

. SUN

This illustration shows the Sun's size in comparison to the star VY Canis Majoris.

A star called VY Canis Majoris is the biggest star anyone knows about. It is not a giant or a supergiant. It is a hypergiant. The term *hyper* comes from a Greek word meaning "beyond measure." VY Canis Majoris is nearly two thousand times larger than the Sun. If you could replace the Sun with VY Canis Majoris, it would engulf all the planets in the solar system out to Saturn. If you made a model of the Sun 1 inch (2.54 centimeters) wide, a comparable model of VY Canis Majoris would be a ball 167 feet (51 meters) across.

VY Canis Majoris is also the most luminous star known. Luminosity is a measure of the total amount of light energy put out by a star. VY Canis Majoris is 430,000 times more luminous than the Sun. So it puts out 430,000 times more light energy.

BIG RED

Stars shine because they convert fuel into energy. For most stars, this fuel is hydrogen. By converting hydrogen to helium, stars generate heat and light.

As a star gets older, its hydrogen gets used up. The amount of helium in its core grows larger. With less fuel available, the star is no longer able to send as much energy into space. It becomes like a balloon losing its air.

Gravity then contracts the core of the star. This compression drives up the star's temperature, the same way squeezing a rubber ball tightly in your fist makes it grow warmer. Eventually, the pressure and temperature become so great that the star begins burning its helium. It does this very quickly. This burning makes the core even hotter.

The additional heat causes gases in the outer layers of the star to expand into space. As the gases travel into space, they cool. The star becomes much larger and cooler than it once was. It glows red. We then call the star a red giant. If it grows even bigger, it may become a supergiant or even a hypergiant. But these big stars are very rare.

"*If our Sun were replaced by VY Canis Majoris we could not see it from Earth because Earth would be inside VY Canis Majoris.*"

—*J. T. Maston, American astronomer, 2010*

THE HOTTEST
Stars

The color of a star gives a clue to its temperature. The same is true for a hot piece of metal. The glowing red burner of an electric stove is not as hot as the white filament of a lightbulb. The stove top may be 500°F (260°C). The lightbulb filament is about 4,500°F (2,500°C).

As temperature increases, color changes from red to orange to yellow to white. Finally, if something is hot enough, it glows blue white or even violet. The bluish flame from a welder's torch may be as hot as 6,300°F (3,500°C).

The hottest stars are blue giants. The surface temperature of the Sun is about 10,000°F (5,500°C). A typical blue giant may have a surface temperature of 35,000°F (19,500°C). If a blue giant is hot enough, its light goes beyond violet to ultraviolet. The human eye cannot see ultraviolet light.

Rigel is one of the hottest blue giants known to scientists. It has a surface temperature of about 36,000°F (20,000°C). You can easily see this star without a telescope. It is one of the brightest stars in the constellation Orion *(see diagram page 27)*.

Because they are so large, red giants are very bright stars. This makes them easy to see in the night sky. And their red color also stands out. Betelgeuse is a bright star at the left shoulder of the human figure outlined by the constellation Orion. Betelgeuse is a huge star. Even though it is 500 light-years away, it is still one of the brightest stars in the sky. In fact, it is about ten thousand times more luminous than the Sun.

The large star at the bottom of this photograph is Rigel, a hot blue giant. The surrounding starburst was created by the camera used to take the picture.

The red giant Betelgeuse would extend beyond Jupiter if it were to replace the Sun.

LITTLE STARS AND *Big Stars*

Astronomers use the mass of the Sun as a standard for measuring other stars. We call the measure of the Sun's mass 1 solar mass. Most known stars range from 0.1 to 10 solar masses.

Stars of about the same mass as the Sun resemble it in size and color. Stars with less mass than the Sun are cooler and dimmer. Stars with much more mass are usually much larger, hotter, and brighter. The known upper limit to star size is about 150 times the mass of the Sun.

STARS IN OLD AGE

Red giants, supergiants, and hypergiants are all stars near the end of their lives. They have burned all their hydrogen. They have begun burning their helium, which is heavier than hydrogen. Eventually, the helium runs out as well. So the star begins burning even heavier elements. It burns carbon, which comes from burning helium. It then burns oxygen, which comes from burning carbon, and so on. These last heavy-element-burning stages of a star's life occur very quickly. A typical star has enough hydrogen to last about ten billion years. But once a star starts burning heavier elements, its fuel supply may last only another one thousand years.

As a red giant enters the final stages of its life, its thin, red-glowing atmosphere begins to drift off into space. The inner core, which still contains most of the mass of the original star, slowly shrinks. As it does, it gets hotter. Eventually, most of the elements in the star turn into iron. The star can go no further than this. Fusion stops. The star is like a chunk of coal that has burned into a cinder.

The star has no source of energy left to counterbalance the force of gravity. The star begins to contract rapidly. It grows smaller and denser until the subatomic particles (electrons and neutrons) that make up its core can be

"The term 'giant' pertains not only to the high luminosity [brightness] of these stars, but also to their large geometrical dimensions."

—*George Gamow, Russian astronomer, 1964*

compressed no further. The star may have originally been the size of the Sun. But it has become no larger than Earth. It has become a white dwarf.

GOOD-BYE SUN

As it uses up its hydrogen fuel, the Sun will eventually enter a red giant stage. As it does, its atmosphere will expand into space. The atmosphere will engulf the orbits (paths through space) of Mercury, Venus, and perhaps even Earth. Hundreds of times larger than it is today, the Sun will overwhelm the inner planets (Mercury, Venus, Earth, and Mars) with a flood of red-hot gas. The planets will burn up. This event is at least four billion years in the future.

When our Sun becomes a red giant, several billion years from now, the surface of the Earth will melt from the Sun's intense heat.

MORE *Dwarfs*

Astronomers call a number of very different objects dwarfs. White dwarfs are the remnants of burned-out stars. Brown dwarfs *(below)* are objects that might have become stars, but they never got large enough to have fusion reactions. They never became full-fledged stars. Red dwarfs are ordinary stars, but they are smaller, cooler, and redder than the Sun. Yellow dwarfs are considered average or normal stars. The Sun is a yellow dwarf.

THE AFTERLIFE OF A STAR

After a star burns out, it becomes a white dwarf. White dwarfs may be no larger than Earth. But they are still very massive. A white dwarf still contains almost all the material from the original star. But this material is compacted into a very small space, like a handful of snow pressed tightly into a small snowball.

White dwarfs are extremely hot. The surface temperature of a white dwarf may be greater than that of the Sun. White dwarfs shine with an intense blue white light. After billions of years, they eventually cool off entirely. They become dark, cold, planet-sized cinders.

5 THE MOST EARTHLIKE Extrasolar Planet

This illustration shows the landscape of Gliese 581d, an Earthlike planet beyond the solar system.

$\mathcal{F}$OR HUNDREDS OF YEARS, ASTRONOMERS

HAVE WONDERED IF THERE ARE OTHER PLANETS LIKE OUR OWN. A

PLANET CALLED GLIESE 581D IS THE CLOSEST THEY'VE FOUND YET.

Astronomers first discovered planets around the star Gliese 581 (lower right) in 2007.

Scientists are pretty sure they know how our solar system formed. About 4.6 billion years ago, the Sun was surrounded by a disk of dust and gas left over from its formation. As the disk rotated, it got flatter and thinner, just as pizza dough gets flatter and thinner as a pizza maker spins it around.

Particles of dust in the spinning disk stuck together and formed clumps. Small clumps stuck together and made bigger ones. The bigger the clumps got, the more mass they had. The more mass they had, the more gravity they made. The more gravity they had, the more other clumps they attracted. Eventually, some of the clumps got to be very big. They became planets.

This illustration places the planets of the solar system and their moons close together to show how they compare in size. If planets formed around the Sun, it seems likely that planets also formed around other stars.

What's in a *Name?*

Objects in space get their names in many different ways. Some names, such as the Crab Nebula and Horsehead Nebula, are simple descriptions. The names tell what the objects look like. Some names come from different languages. Ancient Arab astronomers noticed a star that seemed to follow the star cluster Pleiades in the sky. The astronomers named the star Aldebaran, which means "the follower" in Arabic. Many objects in space are named for characters from Greek and Roman mythology. Examples include the planet Neptune. It is named for the Roman god of the sea.

The pulsar PSR B1257+12 has a much less interesting name. PSR simply stands for pulsating source of radio. The numbers following PSR indicate where this particular pulsar is in the sky. The star Gliese 581 is named for a catalog of stars compiled by German astronomer Wilhelm Gliese. It is star number 581 in the catalog. Gliese 581b was the first planet found orbiting the star. Gliese 581c was the second planet found orbiting the star. Gliese 581d was the third. There is no Gliese 581a, since the designation "a" is reserved for the star itself. If astronomers discover another planet orbiting the star, they will name it Gliese 581e.

Finding Other Worlds

There is no reason that something similar couldn't have happened around other stars. There is no reason that other stars shouldn't have planets. But a planet around a distant star is very difficult to see. Stars are huge objects that give off light. Planets are small and dark. They can be seen only by the light they reflect.

Since it is almost impossible to see a planet orbiting a distant star, scientists have to use indirect methods. One method is to detect the effect a planet has on the star it orbits. As a planet travels around a star, its gravity tugs on the star slightly. This tugging makes the star wobble a little. When astronomers detect a star wobbling, they know that a planet is causing the wobble.

A star can reveal the existence of a planet in another way. Sometimes during its orbit, a planet passes between its star and Earth. When this happens, the planet blocks some of the light coming from the star. Astronomers can see the star dim very slightly. They know that a planet has crossed its path.

ON THE RIGHT TRACK

In the 1980s, astronomers finally proved that some stars have at least one object orbiting them. In most cases, these objects are very large. Most are many times bigger than Jupiter, the largest planet in our solar system. Astronomers realized that these objects were not planets. Instead, they were brown dwarfs, objects that never got large enough to become stars. Brown dwarfs were not the planets astronomers were looking for. But their discovery showed that scientists were on the right track.

PLANETS AT LAST

In the 1990s, Swiss astronomers Michel Mayor and Didier Queloz examined 150 stars. In 1995 they finally found a planet orbiting the star 51 Pegasi. It was the first planet known to orbit a star similar to the Sun. The planet is seven

This illustration shows the planet orbiting 51 Pegasi. The planet is probably a hot ball of molten rock.

In this illustration, the large object at right is the planet orbiting 70 Virginis. 70 Virginis itself is the bright star at left. It shines from behind one of the planet's moons.

times wider than Earth, but it is far too small to be a brown dwarf. It orbits very close to 51 Pegasi. It is only about 4.3 million miles (7 million km) away. It takes only four days for the planet to orbit the star.

Heat from 51 Pegasi makes the planet extremely hot. Its surface temperature is more than 1,830°F (1,000°C). This is hot enough to bring rock to a red heat and to melt lead, tin, or silver. The planet is probably a ball of nearly molten (melted) rock and iron. It has seven times the surface gravity of Earth. If you could stand on the planet's surface, you would weigh seven times what you do on Earth.

In January 1996, U.S. astronomers Geoffrey Marcy and Paul Butler discovered another solar system like our own. They discovered a planet orbiting the star 70 Virginis. It is a star similar to our Sun. The planet has a mass about nine times that of Jupiter. This size means that the planet might be a brown dwarf. It orbits 70 Virginis at about half the distance between Earth and the Sun. Its surface may be about 185°F (85°C). This temperature is below the boiling point of water. So life may be able to exist on the planet. Geoffrey Marcy thinks the planet might have oceans and rainfall. Other astronomers think it might be a giant gas planet, with no solid surface on which water can collect. No one knows for sure.

Since the mid-1990s, scientists have discovered more than four hundred extrasolar (outside our solar system) planets. This number is continually growing. As astronomers gain experience finding planets, they will be able to detect smaller and smaller worlds, perhaps even worlds like Earth.

New Earths?

The discovery of so many extrasolar planets has been exciting. But what astronomers especially hope to find is evidence of planets like Earth—that is, planets capable of supporting life.

The first Earthlike planet they found orbits a star called CoRoT-7. Astronomers discovered the planet in 2009. It is only 1.7 times the diameter (width) of Earth. Called CoRoT-7b, the planet is probably made of metal and rock, like Earth. But that's where the resemblance ends. The planet is more than twenty times closer to its star than Earth is to the Sun. The temperature on the surface is between 3,300 and 4,700°F (1,800 and 2,600°C). The planet is most likely covered in red-hot molten lava. The atmosphere of CoRoT-7b is probably deadly. In addition to oxygen, it may hold potassium and sodium. On the night side of the planet, the side that faces away from the star, it might rain

Astronomers named the star CoRoT-7 for the CoRoT satellite (above). From its orbit around Earth, the satellite looks for extrasolar planets.

liquid iron, aluminum, and silicon. CoRoT-7b is not the sort of place anyone would want to go on vacation.

ALMOST EARTH

Scientists found a close match to Earth in December 2009. It is a planet called GJ 1214b. At first glance, it does not seem very much like our world. For one thing, it is 2.7 times larger than Earth. It also orbits very close to its small, dim, red star. It is seventy times closer to its star than Earth is to the Sun.

Although its star is not as hot as the Sun, GJ 1214b still gets a lot of heat. The surface temperature is around 390°F (200°C). This would normally be much too hot for liquid water to exist. Any water on the planet would normally boil and turn into gas. But GJ 1214b has a thick, heavy atmosphere. It might be 125 miles (200 km) deep. The temperature at which water boils depends on the air pressure above it. Higher pressure gives water a higher boiling point. The heavy atmosphere pressing down on GJ 1214b might allow liquid water to exist on its surface, despite the high temperature.

If GJ 1214b has liquid water, the planet might be almost entirely covered by a vast ocean. It would not be an ocean you'd care to swim in, though. The water would be almost twice as hot as water boiling on your kitchen stove. Underneath the ocean, the planet itself might be made mostly of water ice, with a small core of rock and metal.

EVEN CLOSER

Perhaps the best match to Earth anyone has yet found is a planet called Gliese 581d. Astronomers discovered it in 2007. It orbits very near a red dwarf star. Gliese 581d is five times closer to its star than Earth is to the Sun. Gliese 581d circles the star once every 66.8 days.

The star itself is called Gliese 581. It is only about one-third the size and mass of the Sun. Gliese 581 is much dimmer too. It is only 0.2 percent as luminous as the Sun.

At least four planets orbit the little star. One is a Neptune-sized gas giant. Gas giants are made mostly of gas and liquid. This kind of planet is too cold to support life. Another planet is a rocky world only slightly larger than Earth. But the planet orbits very close to the star. It may be too hot for life.

"Do there exist many worlds, or is there but a single world? This is one of the most noble and exalted [important] questions in the study of Nature."
—Albertus Magnus, English philosopher, 1200s

Gliese 581c was the second of four planets discovered around Gliese 581. It is slightly larger than Earth and rotates very near its star. It is probably too hot to support life.

For a planet to support life, it must be neither too hot nor too cold for water to exist in liquid form. It must be close enough to its star to keep living things warm but not so close as to burn them up. Astronomers call this distance the Goldilocks Zone. The name is based on the famous fairy tale in which Goldilocks rejects porridge that is too hot and too cold in favor of porridge that is "just right." Gliese 581d lies in the Goldilocks Zone. Its conditions are just right for life.

Astronomers think Gliese 581d might have a rocky core with a thick layer of ice above it. On top of this layer may be an ocean of liquid water. The planet also has an atmosphere. An atmosphere around a planet creates a "greenhouse effect." Heat from its star warms the surface of the planet. The atmosphere keeps heat from escaping back out into space, much like the

Bacteria and other microorganisms on Earth live in extreme conditions, such as this hot spring in Yellowstone National Park in Wyoming. Perhaps organisms could also live in extreme conditions on other planets.

glass roof of a greenhouse keeps heat trapped inside. The greenhouse effect causes the surface of a planet to become much warmer than it would be if its atmosphere didn't exist. For instance, without the greenhouse effect of its atmosphere, Earth would be a chilly −0.4°F (−18°C).

Gliese 581d might be capable of supporting life. But this isn't to say that it would be a very nice world to live on. Because Gliese 581d orbits so close to its star, it does not rotate. Gliese 581's strong gravity keeps one side of the planet always facing the star. That side of the planet is probably very hot. The side facing away from the star is probably extremely cold. Winds blowing through the planet's dense atmosphere might even out the temperatures somewhat, making the hot side a little cooler and the cold side a little warmer. Still, the planet's temperatures are probably very extreme. The night side is always dark.

But Earth has some places with even more extreme conditions. Earth has hot springs, acid pools, volcanic vents, and deep ice. Plants and animals manage to survive in all these places. So life may have adapted to deal with the harsh conditions on Gliese 581d as well. But if life does exist there, it is very different from life on Earth.

The largest known galaxy sits at the center of the Abell 2029 galaxy cluster. The galaxy is in the constellation Serpens.

$\mathcal{G}$ALAXIES ARE VAST COLLECTIONS OF STARS. THE SUN AND ALL THE STARS WE CAN SEE IN THE SKY ARE PART OF A GALAXY CALLED THE MILKY WAY. THE MILKY WAY IS A COLLECTION OF 200 TO 400 BILLION STARS. THEY SWIRL TOGETHER LIKE CREAM STIRRED INTO A CUP OF HOT COFFEE.

Astronomers used special cameras to create this image of the Milky Way. The center of the galaxy is the bright white area at center right.

If you could see all the Milky Way at once, from some vast distance beyond it, it would resemble a fried egg. It has a bulbous center surrounded by a thick, flat disk. The center is made of millions of stars crowded together. The disk is composed of graceful arms that spiral out from the central bulge like a pinwheel. The arms, too, are made of millions of stars. Buried deep within one of those spiral arms, about two-thirds of the way from the central bulge, is the Sun and its planets.

THE
Milky Way

The word *galaxy* comes from a Greek word meaning "milk." The ancient Greeks coined the name *galaxy* because they thought our own galaxy looked like a stream of milk pouring through the night sky. When we call our galaxy the Milky Way, we are using the same description the Greeks did. In modern times, we know that the Milky Way is a vast collection of billions of stars. We call other such collections of stars galaxies too.

BIGGER THAN BIG

The Milky Way is a very big galaxy. It is bigger than its nearest neighbor, the Andromeda Galaxy. But it is a dwarf compared to the biggest galaxy known to astronomers. This is a galaxy called IC 1101. Like the Milky Way, it is a spiral galaxy. But it is at least sixty times larger. The Milky Way is about 100,000 light-years across. IC 1101 is from 5.6 to 6 million light-years across. It is home to as many as 100 trillion stars. The Milky Way contains 200 to 400 billion stars.

IC 1101 is one billion light-years from Earth. The light we see from IC 1101 left that galaxy one billion years ago. When the light started on its way, simple plants were the only life on Earth. Because IC 1101 is so far away, it is hard for scientists to study it in detail. In even the best telescopes, it looks like a fuzzy oval blob.

How did this galaxy get to be so big? Scientists aren't sure. But IC 1101 sits in the middle of a very large cluster of smaller galaxies. It may have grown large by "eating" other galaxies in the cluster. As they merged with IC 1101, it grew larger and larger. There may be no limit to how large IC 1101 will become.

TYPES AND SHAPES

Galaxies come in many different sizes and shapes. Astronomer Edwin Hubble divided the different shapes into categories in 1936. Spiral galaxies, such as the Milky Way, are the most familiar shape. Some spiral galaxies, such as the Andromeda Galaxy, have a round central bulge. Other galaxies, such as the Milky Way, are barred spirals. In barred spirals, the central bulge is bar shaped.

Spiral galaxies are not the most common type of galaxy. Only about 15 percent of the galaxies known to

Right: *U.S. astronomer Edwin Hubble studied galaxies in the mid-twentieth century.*
Below: *The Andromeda Galaxy is a spiral galaxy.*

astronomers are spirals. About 65 percent of all galaxies are small and globelike. These galaxies are known as dwarf elliptical galaxies. They are shaped more like basketballs or hamburger buns than flat disks.

About 5 percent of galaxies are giant elliptical galaxies. They are very similar to dwarf elliptical galaxies. But as their name implies, they are much larger. They can be even larger than spirals.

Another 15 percent of known galaxies are irregular galaxies. The Large Magellanic Cloud is a good example of an irregular galaxy. It looks like a splash of spilled milk. It is one of a pair of small irregular galaxies that orbit the Milky Way.

MAKE YOUR OWN
Spiral Galaxy

The Milky Way is a spiral galaxy. With a large bowl, water, a large spoon, and food coloring, you can make a model of the galaxy.

Fill the bowl with water. Stir the water gently in just one direction with the spoon. Stirring will make the water in the bowl rotate. Stop stirring and immediately dribble a few drops of food coloring into the water. Quickly dribble them at different distances from the center of the bowl. Each drop will form its own spiral arm. The length and the speed of each arm's rotation will depend on its distance from the center of the bowl. As the water rotates, the food coloring will look more and more like a spiral galaxy.

AMAZING GALAXIES

Most galaxies fall neatly into one of the basic forms: spiral, barred spiral, elliptical, or irregular. But some take more unusual shapes. The unusual galaxies include ring and rattail galaxies.

Although the universe is huge, and hundreds and sometimes millions of light-years separate galaxies, they do sometimes run into one another. The stars in colliding galaxies rarely hit one another, however, because they are spread so far apart. The galaxies usually slip right through one another without any individual stars colliding. But the gravitational pull of each galaxy can have a powerful effect on another galaxy. As the galaxies pass through one another, they pull and distort one another into unusual shapes.

This picture shows NGC 1316, a giant elliptical galaxy about 75 million light-years from Earth.

If a small galaxy passes right through the middle of a larger one, it might punch out the center of the larger galaxy, like making a doughnut by cutting out the center of a circle of dough. This may be how ring galaxies form. They look a little like glowing Hula-hoops.

If the collision is a glancing, or sideways, one, two spiral galaxies might actually "unwind" each other. Their arms will stretch off into space like long streamers. Such galaxies are called rattail galaxies because they look like they have long, skinny tails.

Left: *The ring galaxy AM 0644-741 is 300 million light-years from Earth.*
Right: *NGC 4038 is a rattail galaxy.*

JETTING GALAXIES

Some galaxies look like pinwheels spinning on a flaming axis, or central shaft. These galaxies shoot out powerful jets of energy millions of light-years into space. Astronomers call these jetting galaxies. Astronomers think the jets of energy come from supermassive black holes.

All galaxies have black holes. A black hole is the result of a collapsing star. When a star collapses, it usually becomes a neutron star or a pulsar. But if the star is big enough, the collapse might not stop there. As the star collapses on itself, it gets denser. The denser it gets, the more gravity it produces. The more gravity it produces, the faster it collapses. Eventually its gravity becomes so powerful that even light can't escape. The collapsing star has turned into a black hole.

Ordinary black holes absorb small space objects, such as dust, meteorites, and asteroids. This matter releases energy as it falls into the black hole. A supermassive black hole is an extremely large black hole. Instead of absorbing only small objects such as dust and meteorites, supermassive black holes eat whole stars. A supermassive black hole may be 100 billion or even 1 trillion times as heavy as the Sun.

Supermassive black holes emit huge quantities of energy. The energy shoots out in powerful jets from the top and the bottom of the galaxy. That's why galaxies that contain supermassive black holes are called jetting galaxies.

"How could we hope to detect a black hole, as by its very definition it does not emit any light? It might seem a bit like looking for a black cat in a coal cellar."

—Stephen Hawking, British physicist, 1988

This illustration shows a jetting galaxy. Energy shoots out from a supermassive black hole at the galaxy's center.

QUASARS

In the 1960s, astronomers discovered some powerful radio waves in the universe. But when they looked for the source, all they could find were bright, starlike objects. Astronomers named these objects quasi-stellar radio sources, or quasars for short. (*Quasi-stellar* means "starlike.")

Scientists at first thought that quasars were strange stars within our own galaxy. They later realized that quasars must be very far away. Modern astronomers believe that quasars are the intensely bright cores of far-distant galaxies.

Something causes the cores of these galaxies to emit incredible amounts of energy. Some scientists think that supermassive black holes might be the cause. Matter falling into the supermassive black holes might be the source of the radio waves detected on Earth. But no one knows for sure.

A quasar may eventually quiet down when most of the available stars, dust, and gas at the center of its galaxy are used up. A black hole at the center of our Milky Way may once have been a quasar. But it now emits much less energy, since it has fewer stars and less gas to feed it.

"Quasars . . . may be the colossal explosions of young galaxies, the mightiest events in the history of the universe since the Big Bang [the event that created the universe] itself."

—Carl Sagan, American astronomer, 1980

A quasar as imagined by an artist. Quasars give off massive amounts of energy.

7 THE SCULPTOR
Supercluster

The Sculptor Supercluster is the largest of the universe's more than 10 million superclusters.

OF ALL THE THINGS IN THE UNIVERSE, THE
BIGGEST STRUCTURE ANYONE HAS EVER FOUND IS THE SCULPTOR
SUPERCLUSTER. IT IS A COLLECTION OF BILLIONS AND BILLIONS OF
INDIVIDUAL GALAXIES.

Just as stars gather to form galaxies, galaxies gather to form groups and clusters. The Milky Way is in a neighborhood of galaxies known as the Local Group. This group has more than forty members.

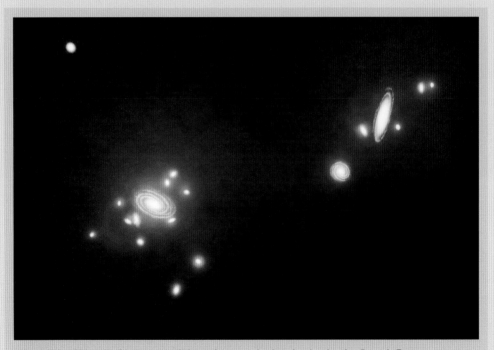

The Milky Way (left) is one of three large spiral galaxies in the Local Group.

ANDROMEDA
GALAXY
The Andromeda
Galaxy is about 2.9
million light-years
from the Sun.

MILKY WAY

SUN

This diagram shows some of the different galaxy members of the Local Group.

The Milky Way is the most massive galaxy in the group, followed by the Andromeda Galaxy and the Triangulum Galaxy. All three are giant spiral galaxies. Most of the rest of the galaxies in the Local Group are small galaxies that orbit either the Milky Way or Andromeda. The galaxies that form the Local Group are locked together by gravitation.

Groups of galaxies also cluster together. The Local Group is part of a cluster with five other groups. Some clusters contain as many as one thousand galaxies.

TRIANGULUM GALAXY
At 3 million light-years from the Sun, the Triangulum Galaxy is the most distant member of the Local Group.

LARGE MAGELLANIC CLOUD
The Large Magellanic Cloud orbits the Milky Way.

THE LOCAL GROUP
The Milky Way and its neighbors as seen from a location about 700,000 light-years from the Sun. The nearest galaxy is the Large Magellanic Cloud. The Local Group has about forty members, but not all show up in this picture. The Sun is marked by a red dot. In reality it would be invisibly small from this distance.

SUPERCLUSTERS

Clusters in turn gather with one another to form even larger clusters. These formations are called superclusters. The cluster that contains the Local Group belongs to the Virgo Supercluster.

The Virgo Supercluster is made up of at least one hundred groups and clusters. It covers an area of space 110 million light-years across. The galaxies that make up the Virgo Supercluster are all tied together by gravity. The galaxies slowly swarm around within the supercluster like bees in a hive.

The Local Group is shown on the far right in this artist's illustration. It is one of many groups that combine to form the Virgo Supercluster.

The universe contains at least 10 million superclusters. Each may contain as many as ten thousand galaxies. Each galaxy may contain up to 100 billion stars.

One hundred superclusters are found within 100 billion light-years of Earth. The biggest of these that we know of is the Sculptor Supercluster. It is one billion light-years from Earth. The Sculptor Supercluster contains many thousands of individual galaxy groups. It stretches over 250 million light-years of space. That's almost 15.8 trillion times the distance between Earth and the Sun.

> "The cosmos [universe] is all that is or ever was or ever will be. Our feeblest contemplations of the Cosmos stir us—— there is a tingling in the spine, a catch in the voice, a faint sensation, as if a distant memory, or falling from a height. We know we are approaching the greatest of mysteries."
>
> —Carl Sagan, American astronomer, 1980

THE UNIVERSE

All the millions of separate superclusters are loosely connected together in a vast web. Together they make up something even bigger. This is the universe itself. It's the biggest thing there is. The word *universe* means "everything." And that's exactly what the universe contains. It includes *everything*: every atom, every molecule, every planet, every star, and every galaxy. It includes every grain of dust, every tree, every animal, and everybody, including you.

The universe contains 30 to 70 sextillion stars. (A sextillion is written with the number 1 followed by fifty-one 0s.) These stars form more than 80 billion galaxies. These galaxies form superclusters that stretch out in long strings. If you could see the whole universe at one time, it would look a little like a sponge

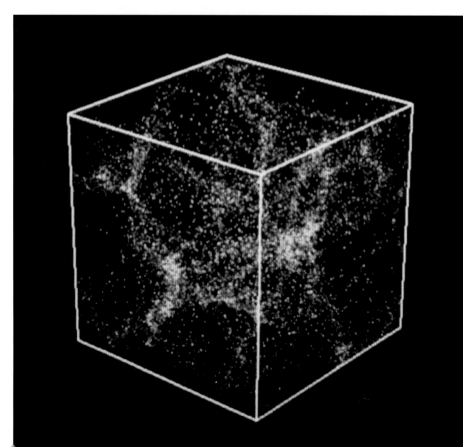

This computer model of a portion of the universe shows the loose connections between different superclusters.

or spiderweb. The structure of the universe is sometimes also compared to foam. The long strings of superclusters surround gigantic, empty holes that look like bubbles. The biggest of these bubbles is 100 billion light-years across.

Is there anything bigger than the universe? Scientists aren't sure. They can see only so far with their telescopes. So far, the limit is the incredible distance of 46.5 billion light-years. Scientists refer to the universe they can study as the "observable universe." The actual universe may be much bigger than that. Some astronomers estimate that the entire universe may be 100 billion trillion to 100 trillion trillion times bigger than the one we can see.

WHERE DID IT ALL Come From?

Many astronomers study how the universe came to be. These astronomers are called cosmogonists. Cosmogony is the study of the origins of the universe.

Most cosmogonists believe the universe was born in an event called the big bang. Before the big bang, there was nothing. Neither time nor space existed. After the big bang, there was everything.

According to scientists, the universe began about 13.7 billion years ago. It began with a "singularity," or single thing. Scientists are not sure what this singularity was. Whatever it was, it was probably almost infinitely (immeasurably) small, infinitely hot, and infinitely dense. No one knows where it came from or what caused it to appear.

What scientists are sure of is that the singularity was unstable. Almost as soon as it appeared, it began to expand—very rapidly. This rapid expansion is called the big bang.

After the big bang, the universe was a mass of energy and random particles. After a few seconds, all the basic chemical elements took form. But it took 300 million years for these elements to become stars and galaxies. The Sun was not born until 5 billion years after the big bang.

Our universe has never stopped expanding. All the stars and all the galaxies in the universe are slowly moving away from one another. So it is accurate to say that the big bang is still going on.

"There must have been an instant in time . . . when the entire Universe was contained in a single point in space. The Universe must have been born in this single violent event which came to be known as the "Big Bang.""

—National Aeronautics and Space Administration, 2010

This illustration shows the web of the universe.

TIMELINE

ca. 400 B.C.	Greek philosopher Democritus proposes that the Milky Way consists of stars like the Sun.
1054	Chinese astronomers observe the supernova responsible for the creation of the Crab Nebula.
1572	Danish astronomer Tycho Brahe notices a "new star" in the constellation Cassiopeia. It is really an exploding star, which he calls a nova.
1610	Italian scientist Galileo Galilei is the first person to use a telescope to study the night sky.
1936	U.S. astronomer Edwin Hubble classifies galaxies according to shape: spiral, barred spiral, elliptical, or irregular.
1963	Astronomers first identify quasars.
1967	British astronomers Jocelyn Bell and Anthony Hewish discover radio pulses coming from pulsars.
1987	A supernova explodes in the Large Magellanic Cloud. It is the first supernova in almost four hundred years that can be seen with the naked eye.
1990	The United States places the Hubble Space Telescope in orbit. The telescope is named for astronomer Edwin Hubble.
1992	Scientists notice that PSR B1257+12 has an uneven pulse. They determine that planets must be orbiting the pulsar.
1995	Astronomers Michel Mayor and Didier Queloz find a planet orbiting 51 Pegasi. It is the first planet found to orbit a star similar to the Sun.
2009	Astronomers discover the Earthlike planets CoRoT-7b and GJ 1214.
2010	The Kepler Space Telescope discovers more than three hundred new extrasolar planets in six months.

CHOOSE AN EIGHTH WONDER

Now that you've read *Seven Wonders beyond the Solar System,* do a little research to choose an eighth wonder. You may enjoy working with a friend.

To start your research, look at some of the websites and books listed on the following pages. Use the Internet and library books to find more information. What other things beyond our solar system are wondrous? Think about things that
- ***Have been newly discovered***
- ***Show evidence of life beyond our solar system***
- ***Are extremely large or extremely small***

You might even try gathering photos and writing your own chapter on the eighth wonder.

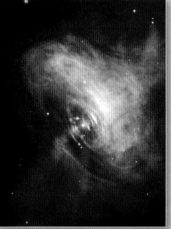

8

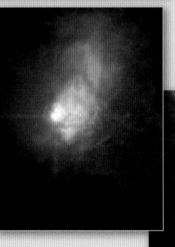

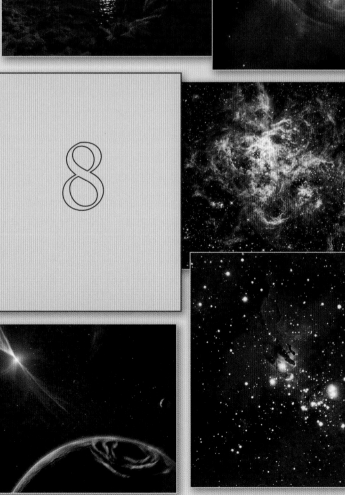

GLOSSARY AND PRONUNCIATION GUIDE

atmosphere: the layer of gases that surrounds a planet or a star

atom: a small particle of matter consisting of a nucleus with one or more electrons orbiting it

black hole: a region of space whose gravity is so strong that nothing can escape from it

brown dwarf: a large planetlike body that is too small for nuclear fusion, which would make it a true star, but large enough to glow from the heat produced by its own gravity

cluster: a collection of groups of galaxies

constellation: a group of stars that cover a particular region of the night sky. Ancient people thought that certain constellations looked like outlines of figures, animals, and objects and named them accordingly.

density: a measure of the amount of mass within a space or an object

extrasolar: outside our solar system

fusion: the merging of the nuclei of two atoms into one

galaxy: a collection of billions of stars. Some galaxies, like our Milky Way, form giant spirals, while others have different shapes.

gas giant: a planet that consists mostly of gas and liquid, with only a tiny rocky core. Jupiter and Saturn are gas giants within our solar system.

giant star: an unusually large star, much bigger than the Sun

gravitational contraction: the slow contraction, or shrinking, of clouds of dust, a planet, or a star due to the pull of its own gravity

gravity: the mutual attraction of bodies that have mass

hydrogen: the simplest and most abundant element in the universe

hypergiant: an unusually large star, much bigger than a supergiant

jetting galaxy: a galaxy with enormous jets of energy shooting from its center. The jets are probably produced by giant black holes.

light-year: the distance light travels in one year—approximately 5.88 trillion miles (9.46 trillion km)

luminosity: a measure of the light energy of an object such as a star

mass: the amount of stuff something is made of

nebula: a cloud of dust and gas in space or surrounding a star

nebulae (NEHB-yoo-lee): the plural of nebula

neutron: one of the basic particles inside an atom

neutron star: a small dense ball left over after a star collapses or explodes

nova: an exploding star

nucleus: the center of an atom

orbit: to circle around something

pulsar: a rotating neutron star that produces regular pulses of radio energy

quasar (KWAY-zahr): a galaxy that emits a tremendous amount of energy, probably caused by a giant black hole

red giant: an old star whose surface layers have expanded to many times the size of the original star

ring galaxy: a galaxy shaped like a circle, with an empty center. Ring galaxies probably result from collisions with other galaxies.

rotate: to spin around an axis, or a centerline

star: a huge round object in space that produces light, heat, and other kinds of energy

subatomic: relating to the particles inside atoms

supercluster: a cluster of galaxy clusters

supergiant: a very large star, much larger than a giant

supernova: a star that explodes with unusual violence

universe: everything there is

white dwarf: a planet-sized star with a mass roughly equal to that of the Sun and with a very high density

Source Notes

9 SpaceQuotations.com, "Eyes Turned Skyward: The Stars," SpaceQuotations.com, 2010, http://www.spacequotations.com/stars.html (March 4, 2010).

13 Hubblesite, "Hubble's Panoramic Portrait of a Vast Star-Forming Region," Hubblesite, July 26, 2001, http://hubblesite.org/newscenter/archive/releases/2001/21/image/a/ (March 4, 2010).

21 SpaceQuotations.com, "Eyes Turned Skyward: The Stars."

23 William K. Hartmann and Ron Miller, *Cycles of Fire* (New York: Workman, 1987), 104.

26 Ibid., 48.

28 S. Jocelyn Bell Burnell, "Little Green Men, White Dwarfs or Pulsars?" Cosmic Search, 2004, http://www.bigear.org/vol1no1/burnell.htm (March 13, 2010).

34 J. T. Maston, personal correspondence with author, March 4, 2010.

37 George Gamow, *A Star Called the Sun* (New York: Bantam Books, 1964), 134.

46 Martin Greenberg, *Travelers of Space* (New York: Gnome Press, 1951), 5.

48 SpaceQuotations.com, "Eyes Turned Skyward: Astronomy," SpaceQuotations.com, http://www.spacequotations.com/astronomyquotes.html (February 12, 2010).

59 Stephen Hawking, *A Brief History of Time* (New York: Bantam Books, 1988), 96–97.

61 Carl Sagan, *Cosmos* (New York: Random House, 1980), 249.

67 Ibid., 4.

69 National Aeronautics and Space Administration, "The Big Bang," NASA Science Astrophysics, 2010, http://nasascience.nasa.gov/astrophysics/what-powered-the-big-bang (March 28, 2010).

SELECTED BIBLIOGRAPHY

Associated Press. "Distant Galaxy Found to Be Largest Known." *New York Times*, March 13, 1987. http://www.nytimes.com/1987/03/13/us/distant-galaxy-found-to-be-largest-known.html?pagewanted=1 (March 22, 2010).

Ferris, Timothy. *Galaxies*. New York: Stewart, Tabori and Chang, 1982.

Firsoff, V. A. *Life among the Stars*. London: Allan Wingate, 1974.

Fradin, Dennis Brindell. *The Planet Hunters*. New York: Simon and Schuster, 1997.

Hartmann, William K. *Astronomy: The Cosmic Journey*. Belmont, CA: Wadsworth Publishing, 1985.

Hawking, Stephen. *A Brief History of Time*. New York: Bantam Books, 1988.

Littmann, Mark. *Planets Beyond*. New York: John Wiley and Sons, 1988.

Macvey, John W. *Alone in the Universe?* New York: Macmillan, 1963.

Madrigal, Alexis. "New Telescope Captures Dazzling Image of Orion Nebula." *Wired Science*. February 10, 2010. http://www.wired.com/wiredscience/2010/02/vista-orion/ (March 22, 2010).

Moore, Patrick. *The Atlas of the Universe*. Chicago: Rand McNally, 1970.

Sagan, Carl. *Cosmos*. New York: Random House, 1980.

Shapley, Harlow. *Galaxies*. Cambridge, MA: Harvard University Press, 1961.

Shiga, David. "Hints of Structure beyond the Visible Universe." *New Scientist*, June 10, 2008. http://www.newscientist.com/article/dn14098-hints-of-structure-beyond-the-visible-universe.html (March 22, 2010).

Ward, Peter D., and Donald Brownlee. *Rare Earth*. New York: Copernicus, 2000.

FURTHER READING AND WEBSITES

Books

Asimov, Isaac. *Astronomy Projects*. Strongsville, OH: Gareth Stevens, 2005. Recently updated, this title was authored by acclaimed science writer Isaac Asimov. The book describes astronomy experiments and projects that young people can do with simple materials.

Bortz, Fred. *Astrobiology*. Minneapolis: Lerner Publications Company, 2008. This title showcases the field of astrobiology—the study of how life developed on Earth and how it could similarly exist on other planets.

Butts, Ellen R, and Joyce R.. Schwartz. *Carl Sagan*. Minneapolis: Twenty-First Century Books, 2001. Learn more about the well-known American astronomer Carl Sagan in this biography.

Dickenson, Terrance. *Exploring the Night Sky*. Richmond Hill, ON: Firefly Books, 1987. In this easy guide, readers will learn about many amazing things in the night sky—all of them visible from their own backyard.

Einspruch, Andrew. *Mysteries of the Universe*. Washington, DC: National Geographic Children's Books, 2006. How do astronomers find out what the universe is like? How do they discover new stars and galaxies? This book explains how scientists explore space.

Fleisher, Paul. *The Big Bang*. Minneapolis: Twenty-First Century Books, 2006. Explore the theory of the big bang in this thorough introduction to the topic.

Johnson, Rebecca L. *Satellites*. Minneapolis: Lerner Publications Company, 2006. Read more about the thousands of satellites that circle Earth and discover their many uses.

McPherson, Stephanie Sammartino. *Stephen Hawking*. Minneapolis: Twenty-First Century Books, 2007. This book tells the life story of the British physicist who produced groundbreaking work on the big bang theory. He also brought astronomy to the public with easy-to-read books.

Miller, Ron. *Robot Explorers*. Minneapolis: Twenty-First Century Books, 2008. Ride along on unmanned missions throughout the solar system.

———. *Stars and Galaxies*. Minneapolis: Twenty-First Century Books, 2006. Miller offers a guide to the many wonders of the universe. Photos and illustrations complement the text.

Silverstein, Alvin, Viriginia Silverstein, and Laura Silverstein Nunn. *Global Warming*. Minneapolis: Twenty-First Century Books, 2009. Well-known science writers Alvin and Virginia Silverstein and Laura Silverstein Nunn explain the complex topic of global warming.

———. *The Universe*. Minneapolis: Twenty-First Century Books, 2009. Take an in-depth look at the worlds beyond our own, exploring classes of stars, the characteristics of the eight planets in our solar system, and the many other celestial bodies in the universe.

Simon, Seymour. *Galaxies*. New York: HarperCollins, 1991. This book by revered children's author Seymour Simon describes the many kinds of galaxies that fill the universe, what they are made of, and where they came from.

——. *Stars*. New York: HarperCollins, 1991. This book contains beautiful photographs of stars. Simon's accompanying text explains how stars are formed and describes the many different kinds of stars.

——. *The Universe*. New York: HarperCollins, 2006. What is the universe? Where did it come from? In this book, Simon answers those and many other questions.

Voit, Mark. *Hubble Space Telescope: New Views of the Universe*. New York: Harry N. Abrams, 2000. Since its launch in 1990, the Hubble Space Telescope has revealed many wonders. This book describes those wonders and includes amazing pictures.

Ward, D. J. *Exploring Mars*. Minneapolis: Lerner Publications Company, 2007. Learn amazing facts about Mars in this fast-paced glimpse into the future of science.

Websites

Ask an Astrophysicist
http://imagine.gsfc.nasa.gov/docs/ask_astro/ask_an_astronomer.html
This website from the U.S. National Aeronautics and Space Administration (NASA) provides clear, detailed answers to frequently asked questions about stars, supernovas, black holes, and more.

Astronomy
http://www.astronomy.com
This website is a companion to *Astronomy* magazine.

Astronomy for Kids
http://frontiernet.net/~kidpower/astronomy.html
This site for young people gives information on stars, galaxies, the solar system, and other astronomy topics.

Hubble Space Telescope
http://hubblesite.org/
The official site for the Hubble Space Telescope offers thousands of beautiful photos of objects in space.

Imagine the Universe
http://imagine.gsfc.nasa.gov/docs/science/science.html
At this website, you can find detailed information on stars, black holes, neutron stars, supernovas, and related space topics.

Sky and Telescope
http://www.skypub.com
The official website for *Sky and Telescope* magazine offers a great variety of information on the solar system and beyond.

Star Child
http://starchild.gsfc.nasa.gov/docs/StarChild/StarChild.html
Visit this NASA website to find a variety of information on stars, planets, and the wonders of the universe.

INDEX

About the Author

Hugo Award–winning author and illustrator Ron Miller specializes in books about science. Among his various titles, he has written *The Elements: What You Really Want to Know, Special Effects: An Introduction to Movie Magic,* and *Digital Art: Painting with Pixels.* His favorite subjects are space and astronomy. A postage stamp he created is currently on board a spaceship headed for Pluto. His original paintings can be found in collections all over the world. Miller lives in Virginia.

Photo Acknowledgments

The images in this book are used with the permission of: © Gyro Photography/amanaimagesRF/Getty Images, p. 5; © Robert Gendler/Visuals Unlimited, Inc./Getty Images, p. 6; ESA/NASA/SOHO, p. 7; © Stocktrek Images/Getty Images, pp. 8, 11, 22 (bottom), 71 (middle); © Alex Davidov/Dreamstime.com, p. 9; © Purestock/Getty Images, p. 10; NASA, ESA, M. Robberto (Space Telescope Science Institute/ESA) and the Hubble Space Telescope Orion Treasury Project Team, p. 12; NASA, ESA, J. Hester and A. Loll (Arizona State University), p. 14; NASA/CXC/HST/ASU/J. Hester et al., pp. 15, 71 (top right); © Ron Miller, pp. 16, 17, 25, 26, 29, 31, 33, 38, 39, 40, 41, 42, 44, 45, 49, 60, 61, 62, 64–65, 69, 71 (top left and top middle); NASA and ESA, p. 19 (top); © Mansell/Time & Life Pictures/Getty Images, p. 19 (bottom left); © John Livzey/Photographer's Choice/Getty Images, p. 19 (bottom right); NASA/JPL-Caltech/ESA/CXC/Univ. of Arizona/Univ. of Szeged, p. 20; NASA/JPL-Caltech, pp. 22 (top), 71 (bottom middle); K. Noll (Hubble Heritage PI/STScI), C. Luginbuhl (USNO), F. Hamilton (Hubble Heritage/STScI), p. 23; © Chris Butler/Photo Researchers, Inc., p. 24; © Laura Westlund/Independent Picture Service, p. 27; © John Chumack/Photo Researchers, Inc., pp. 27 (background), 36, 58 (right); © Brian Seed/Time & Life Pictures/Getty Images, p. 28; © Stock Montage/Archive Photos/Getty Images, p. 30 (top); NASA/JSC, p. 30 (bottom); NASA, ESA, and R. Humphreys (University of Minnesota), pp. 32, 71 (bottom left); © Pekka Parviainen/Photo Researchers, Inc., p. 35; © Detlev van Ravenswaay/Photo Researchers, Inc., p. 47; © Wallentine/Dreamstime.com, p. 50; NOAO/Kitt Peak/J. Uson, D. Dale, S. Boughn, J. Kuhn, p. 52; NASA/JPL-Caltech/ESA/CXC/STScI, p. 53; © Jon Brenneis/Time & Life Pictures/Getty Images, p. 55 (top); © David Herraez/Dreamstime.com, p. 55 (bottom); NASA, ESA, and The Hubble Heritage Team (STScI/AURA) with P. Goudfrooij (STScI), p. 57; NASA, ESA, and The Hubble Heritage Team (AURA/STScI) with J. Higdon (Cornell U.) and I. Jordan (STScI), p. 58 (left); © Science Source/Photo Researchers, Inc., p. 59; © Mark Garlick/Photo Researchers, Inc., p. 63; © David Parker/Photo Researchers, Inc., p. 66; © Prof. Vincent Icke/Photo Researchers, Inc., p. 67; © Digital Vision/Getty Images, p. 71 (bottom right).

Front cover: © Ron Miller (top left and top middle); NASA/CXC/HST/ASU/J. Hester et al. (top right); © Stocktrek Images/Getty Images (middle); NASA, ESA, and R. Humphreys (University of Minnesota) (bottom left); NASA/JPL-Caltech (bottom middle); © Digital Vision/Getty Images (bottom right).